PARTSHOTS

PARTY SHOTS

Recipes for Jiggle-iscious Fun

BY Mittie Hellmich

ILLUSTRATIONS BY Stella Lai

CHRONICLE BOOKS

SAN FRANCISCO

Text copyright © 2003 by MITTIE HELLMICH.

Illustrations copyright © 2003 by STELLA LAI.

Library of Congress Cataloging-in-Publication Data:

Hellmich, Mittie, 1960–

Party shots : recipes for jiggle-iscious fun / by Mittie Hellmich ;

illustrations by Stella Lai.

p. cm.

ISBN-10: 0-8118-3950-8

ISBN-13: 978-0-8118-3950-1

1. Cookery (Gelatin) 2. Bartending. I. Title.

TX814.5.G4.H44 2003

641.8'64--dc21

2002156158

Manufactured in China.

Designed by AYAKO AKAZAWA.

Distributed in Canada by RAINCOAST BOOKS

9050 Shaughnessy Street Vancouver, British Columbia V6P 6E5

10 9 8 7 6 5 4 3

CHRONICLE BOOKS LLC

85 Second Street San Francisco, California 94105

www.chroniclebooks.com

GELORAMA

In the ongoing quest for the quick and the potent, gelatin shots are the next wave of cocktail fun.

As cocktail evolution would have it, we've officially advanced from those perfectly balanced, purposely expedient, ounce-and-a-half potent shots of liquid dynamite into a more streamlined, swank, and civil approach. Or, as some would prefer to believe, the Tiki cocktail gods of fun, with their quirky sense of humor, have caused a regression in our cocktail habits, giving us the urge to slam down little brightly colored wiggly cubes of liquored up gelatin.

The colorful fruity stuff that shimmies has been around forever, but exactly when this innocent fun-food turned into a catalyst for bacchanalian party poppers is anyone's guess. There is, however, a vague historical link to the possible conception of the first shooter: Otis Glidden, an ex-Jell-O salesman, produced a gelatin product that included small glass vials of flavoring suspended in alcohol, with the gelatin powder on the side. Alas, this first gelatin shooter, on the shelves for only a year or two, was nipped in the bud once Prohibition came around.

It's easy to imagine the experimentally wild '60s *Electric Kool-Aid Acid Test* era, complete with bathtubs filled with green gelatin, as the perfect cultural segue that takes the fruity '50s gelatin dessert into a potent 2-ounce kinetic cocktail party slider. From there the rest is party-animal legend, linking the gelatin shooter phenomenon to late '70s–early '80s college campus frat parties and rowdy spring-breaks, where it quickly gained popularity.

Now, the gelatin shooter revolution is in full swing. Riding on the wave of the resurgent cocktail craze, there's a huge increase of creative mixology going on right now, and this book is surfing straight into an exploration of the many possibilities of the gelatin cocktail. Beyond the basic vodka and lime or Everclear and sweet cherry shots on a napkin, these are on a higher stratum of new and refined jiggle-iscious fun.

This compendium of innovative elixirs suspended in bouncing lush fruitiness is for anyone looking for a new approach to cocktail party entertaining. So easy to make, these compact cocktails are the libation of choice for those party hosts who would rather samba and circulate than shake cocktails all night. So whether you are planning a funtastic retro party with a gel-atomic twist, or just looking for an excuse to channel overexuberant revelry on spring break, these shimmering, glimmering, high-octane, kinetic cocktail cubes will supply the fun!

> As most of us go blissfully about our business in regards to personal gelatin intake, there is an ongoing battle between Salt Lake City, Utah, and Des Moines, Iowa, to be ranked as the town that consumes the most Jell-O gelatin. Salt Lake City reigned supreme for many years, with lime the most popular flavor. Des Moines has wrestled the title from them once, back in 1999.

GELANETICS 101

THE CHEMISTRY OF PERFECTION

Like every great cocktail, the principles of proportion apply
for a great gelatin shot. We're talking pure alchemy here—
the right balance of ingredients and the correct firmness are
part of the chemistry of perfection. Once you get the formula
basics down, you can transform just about any favorite cocktail into a gelatin shooter.

THE DYNAMICS OF GELATOLOGY

FLAVORED GELATIN

The basic gelatin shot formula is pretty straightforward.
Simply substitute half of the water asked for in the packaged
gelatin directions with a liquor of choice. Dissolve the gelatin
with the hot water and add the alcohol only once the
water/gelatin mixture is cool to the touch. Adding the alcohol
while the mixture is still hot will evaporate it, and at that
point, you might as well squirt on some whipped cream and
call it dessert. Most of the recipes in this book are propor-
tioned to one 3-ounce box of gelatin, making about twenty
gelatin shots that will serve three to four revelers. So if you
are throwing a huge soirée, you will need a few boxes. Simply
multiply the ingredients according to the chosen recipe.

UNFLAVORED GELATIN

Unflavored gelatin, such as the Knox brand, is a different
beast altogether, with the potential for a multitude of
creative adventures. You have a neutral base with which to
infuse with flavors, from fresh juices to intense liqueurs. You
will usually find four ½-ounce envelopes of unflavored gelatin per box, and using two envelopes mixed with two cups of

liquid will make eighteen to twenty (1-ounce) shots. The unflavored gelatin method departs from the norm, in that a half cup of heated juice or alcohol is needed instead of hot water for the best flavor results. You may also need to add sugar to some recipes.

There are quite a few options when it comes to presentation, from 2-ounce party cups, plastic cups, paper nut cups, or Dixie cups for the slider technique, to a more elegant upgrade of shot, cocktail, or cordial glasses, where a spoon is not mandatory, but may be necessary.

If your preference is for firmer, jiggler-style shots that are more of a chewy version than a slider, simply double the flavored or unflavored gelatin amount asked for in the recipe of choice. Your favorite shooter cocktail can be poured into a flat pan and cut into two-inch squares or cut into shapes (stars, hearts, crescent moons, letters of the alphabet) with novelty cookie cutters and served up on a festive plate. Be adventurous with jiggler-style shots, using fun and naughty ice cube trays to mold potent little sculptural shapes that really get the party abuzz.

KINETIC COCKTAILS

When it comes to kinetic sculptural gelatin, there was a study done on lime gelatin, which, when hooked up to an EEG machine, has a wiggle pattern similar to neurological patterns. Now what this indicates in relation to brainwaves after a gelatin shooter, we will let someone else contemplate!

JIGGLY TIPS

Once you substitute your favorite liquor for the cold water, you will find that these perky little shots are very potent—just a few shots per reveler packs quite the wallop. Usually, one part hot water or juice to one part alcohol is a fine ratio, but when using high-proof alcohol, this should be taken into consideration and the amount of alcohol reduced.

• Chill or freeze your alcohol overnight before using to help the gelatin set.

TILT AND SLIDE TECHNIQUE

The basic procedure for shooting back gelatin shots served from a party cup or shot glass: Ring your tongue around the edge to loosen, then slide your tongue under the gelatin and shoot it down.

> **THE ULTIMATE RULE OF THUMB**
> Always eat food before you get involved with drinking shots.

• **HELPFUL FOR SLIDING EFFECTS,** Spray the shooter cups, ice cube trays, or gelatin molds with nonstick cooking spray such as Pam or an olive oil spray. For the ultimate flavor treat, pour aromatic lemon, lime, or orange oil in a small atomizer for a great nonstick way to glide that shot out.

SUSPENDED GELMATION

Aquarium or volcanic eruption anyone? Whether you are structuring an elaborate gelatin mold of Mount Fuji with flora and fauna floating within, or garnishing a few shot glasses, the method is basically the same.

From your favorite fruits to gummy candy, edible flowers, small citrus peels, or mint, all add great flavor and funtastic visuals. Typically you will want to chill your gelatin mixture in

> **SHORT CUT**
> For a quick set, stick the gelatin in the freezer just to thicken, but then transfer to the refrigerator after ten minutes, as freezing gelatin for too long will make it tough and rubbery and hard to shoot.

the refrigerator for at least fifteen minutes (or ten minutes in the freezer for a quick set) to thicken a bit before adding any fruit or other edible ingredient. Fold the chosen fruit or other ingredient into the gelatin in the mixing bowl, then transfer to the pan or gelatin mold. You can also use a toothpick or chopstick to push your gummy fish or raspberry into the slightly set gelatin mixture.

Most fruits work great with gelatin, but some fresh fruits have a natural enzyme that keeps the gelatin from firming and setting, although they can all be used if cooked or canned.

These all contain nongelling agents: Fresh or frozen pineapple, kiwi, figs, mango, guava, papaya, and fresh ginger.

SINKING VERSUS FLOATING FRUITS

Buoyancy (or lack thereof) is the reason behind folding fruits into gelatin once it has chilled and thickened a bit, to keep them suspended in a visually pleasing way. Depending on the visual effect you want, here is a guide to sinking versus swimming.

> You will find that you may want to chew your gelatin shots to get the full flavor experience. Absolutely always chew your shots when there are added suspended ingredients such as olives, gummy worms, raspberries, or mint to avoid choking.

SINKING (LESS BUOYANT): apricots, cherries, fruit cocktail, grapes, peaches, pears, pineapple

FLOATING (MORE BUOYANT): apples, bananas, grapefruit, oranges, raspberries, strawberries

STRATOSPHERIC TECHNIQUES

Now that you have all the basics down to create playful and engaging, cool and fruity, glimmery, shimmery, wiggly, giggly, moving, grooving, happening gelatin shots, you are ready for stirring up a few of these innovative cocktails that you "do" instead of just drink.

FANTASTIC CLASSICS

The classic cocktail gets compact, quick, and potent.

CACTUS QUICKIE

Suavely cut to the chase with these easy, breezy margarita-inspired shots. Made with the classic ingredients, it is complete with a traditional salt rim. OK, so I can't guarantee you won't still get salt on your nose, but I can certainly deliver on that *Agave Aye Carumba!* experience.

SALT RIM **OPTIONAL**
A few lime wedges
½ cup kosher salt in a small bowl

6 ounces water
One 3-ounce package lime gelatin
5 ounces silver tequila
2 ounces Triple Sec (or other orange liqueur)
1 ounce fresh lime juice
1 ounce fresh orange juice
MAKES 20 SHOTS ★ SERVES 3 TO 4

1   **For a Salt Rim:** Run a lime wedge around the rim of each shot cup. Dip each moistened rim in the salt, and set aside.
2   In a small saucepan, bring the water to a boil.
3   Pour the lime gelatin into a medium heatproof bowl and add the boiling water, stirring until the gelatin is dissolved. Let cool.

4 Add the tequila, Triple Sec, lime juice, and orange juice to the cooled mixture, stirring until well combined.

5 Pour mixture into the prepared twenty 2-ounce paper or plastic cups and refrigerate. Chill until firm, 4 to 6 hours.

MOJITO MAMBO

I've taken the classic Cuban Mojito, with its blend of rum, lime juice, mint, and sparkling effervescence, and suspended the refreshing rhythm of flavors in a luscious, lime green gelatin shooter. Whip up a few of these at your next patio party, for an accelerated taste of Havana heaven even Castro couldn't resist.

8 ounces water
One 3-ounce package lime gelatin
5 ounces light rum
2 ounces club soda
1 ounce fresh lime juice
6 to 8 fresh mint leaves, finely chopped (or 2 tablespoons Mint Syrup, page 22)

MAKES 20 SHOTS ★ SERVES 3 TO 4

1 In a small saucepan, bring the water to a boil.
2 Pour the lime gelatin into a medium heatproof bowl and add the boiling water, stirring until the gelatin is dissolved. Let cool.
3 Add the rum, club soda, and lime juice to the cooled mixture, stirring until well combined. Refrigerate in the bowl until thickened and slightly set, about 15 minutes.
4 Fold the mint into the chilled gelatin mixture. Spoon mixture into twenty 2-ounce paper or plastic cups and refrigerate. Chill until firm, 4 to 6 hours.

ATOMIC TONIC

Inspired by the classic summery cocktail-hour libation, I've come up with a contemporary elaboration that enfolds all that sparkling tonic, refreshing lime, and juniper-scented gin, together with the additional luxe of lime sorbet.

6 ounces water
One 3-ounce package lime gelatin
¼ cup lime sorbet
4 ounces gin
2 ounces tonic water
1 ounce fresh lime juice
MAKES 20 SHOTS ★ SERVES 3 TO 4

1   In a small saucepan, bring the water to a boil.
2   Pour the lime gelatin into a medium heatproof bowl and add the boiling water, stirring until the gelatin is dissolved.
3   Add the lime sorbet, stirring until well combined. Let cool.
4   Add the gin, tonic water, and lime juice to the cooled mixture, stirring until well combined.
5   Pour mixture into twenty 2-ounce paper or plastic cups and refrigerate. Chill until firm, 4 to 6 hours.

GELATINI

For those hard-core martini lovers caught up in the urban kinetic fast lane, I've concocted the quickest little power lunch martini this side of Wall Street. If you must go to extremes, use a vermouth atomizer to mist the shots. Of course, if you prefer your 'tinis extra dry, just omit the vermouth altogether. And for a Dirty Gelatini, throw in a tiny splash of olive brine.

8 ounces water
two ½-ounce envelopes unflavored gelatin
8 ounces premium gin or vodka
½ teaspoon dry vermouth
½ teaspoon sweet vermouth

GARNISH **OPTIONAL**
10 green cocktail olives, sliced in half horizontally
··· or ···
¼ cup finely grated lemon zest
MAKES 20 SHOTS ★ SERVES 3 TO 4

1   In a small saucepan, bring the water to a boil.
2   Pour the boiling water into a medium heatproof bowl. Sprinkle the unflavored gelatin into the hot water, stirring until the gelatin is dissolved. Let cool.
3   Add the gin and the dry and sweet vermouths to the cooled mixture, stirring until well combined.

4　Pour mixture into twenty 2-ounce paper or plastic cups and refrigerate for 15 minutes or until slightly set.

5　If garnishing, use a chopstick to push an olive half into the center of each cup, or sprinkle a pinch of lemon zest over the top. Chill until firm, 4 to 6 hours.

COSMOTIQUE

This is a shot as sophisticated and compact as a little red evening bag, but packing a wallop as big as a bookbag! This shimmering, ruby cocktail shooter delivers the same signature cosmo combination of vodka, cranberry, orange, and lime, perfected with a splash of Limoncello liqueur, to give it that extra citrus boost.

8 ounces water
One 3-ounce package cranberry gelatin
5 ounces vodka
1 ounce fresh lime juice
1 ounce Triple Sec (or other orange liqueur)
1 ounce Limoncello liqueur

MAKES 20 SHOTS ★ SERVES 3 TO 4

1 In a small saucepan, bring the water to a boil.
2 Pour the cranberry gelatin into a medium heatproof bowl and add the boiling water, stirring until the gelatin is dissolved. Let cool.
3 Add the vodka, lime juice, Triple Sec, and Limoncello to the cooled mixture, stirring until well combined.
4 Pour mixture into twenty 2-ounce paper or plastic cups and refrigerate. Chill until firm, 4 to 6 hours.

GELL MARY

OK, so you're having a few friends over for Sunday brunch, and the event is just begging for a new, creative approach to the predictable Bloody Mary. Bounce this fiery, spicy shooter onto the scene, complete with the intense heat from wasabi (green Japanese horseradish paste). You can find powdered or prepared wasabi in most Asian markets.

8 ounces V8 juice (or tomato juice)
One 3-ounce package lemon gelatin
6 ounces pepper vodka
1 ounce fresh lime juice
½ teaspoon wasabi paste
A few dashes of Worcestershire sauce
MAKES 20 SHOTS ★ SERVES 3 TO 4

1 In a small saucepan, bring the V8 juice to a low boil.
2 Pour the lemon gelatin into a medium heatproof bowl and add the boiling V8, stirring until the gelatin is dissolved. Let cool.
3 Add the pepper vodka, lime juice, wasabi, and Worcestershire to the cooled mixture, stirring until well combined.
4 Pour mixture into twenty 2-ounce paper or plastic cups and refrigerate. Chill until firm, 4 to 6 hours.

MINT SYRUP

This is a great syrup to have on hand, imparting its refreshing sweet mintiness to many drinks—the possibilities are endless! I like adding it to a fruity iced tea, or any cocktails or gelatin shots asking for mint, such as the Kentucky Julep, Mojito Mambo, or the Monsoon Mango Lassi. You can take it from there.

8 ounces water
½ cup fresh spearmint leaves
1 cup sugar
MAKES 2 CUPS

1 In a small saucepan, bring the water to a boil. Lower the heat and stir in the mint. Cover the pan and remove from the heat. Let stand for an hour or until desired flavor intensity is reached.

2 Strain the mixture into another saucepan. Bring the mint water to a low boil. Reduce the heat to simmer and add the sugar. Stir until the sugar is completely dissolved.

3 Remove the pan from the heat and let the mixture cool completely. Pour into a clean glass jar and cap tightly. Store in the refrigerator and use as needed.

GINGER SYRUP

1 cup water
1 cup sugar
½ cup sliced fresh ginger
MAKES 2 CUPS

1. In a small saucepan, bring the water to a boil. Lower the heat to simmer and add the sugar, stirring until the sugar is completely dissolved.
2. Add the fresh ginger. Cover and remove the pan from the heat. Let stand for an hour or until the desired flavor intensity is reached.
3. Cool completely. Strain the mixture through a fine mesh sieve into a clean glass jar and cap tightly. Store in the refrigerator and use as needed.

SIGNATURE SHOTS

The legendary and notorious cocktails in an abbreviated version.

KENTUCKY JULEP

Southern breezes and lazy days on the veranda are conjured up with this refined adaptation of the mint julep. Kentucky bourbon (Maker's Mark or Knob Creek are two fine choices), sugar, and fragrant, fresh, muddled mint come together in a chilled julep shooter, sure to bring the faint scent of magnolias to your imagination.

8 ounces water
Two ½-ounce envelopes unflavored gelatin
½ cup fresh mint leaves, finely chopped (or 2 tablespoons
    Mint Syrup, page 22)
8 ounces quality bourbon
3 tablespoons superfine sugar

GARNISH **OPTIONAL**
20 fresh mint sprigs
MAKES 20 SHOTS ★ SERVES 3 TO 4

1 In a small saucepan, bring the water to a boil.
2 Pour the boiling water into a medium heatproof bowl and slowly sprinkle the unflavored gelatin into the hot water, stirring until the gelatin is dissolved. Let cool.
3 In a small bowl, mash together the mint, bourbon, and sugar with a wooden spoon until the sugar is dissolved. Add to the cooled mixture, stirring until well combined.
4 Pour mixture into twenty 2-ounce paper or plastic cups and refrigerate. Chill until firm, 4 to 6 hours. Garnish each cup with a mint sprig, if desired, and serve.

ELECTRIC KAMIKAZE

This one's a no-brainer. The classic Kamikaze shot just evolved from liquid to solid, into this potent cube of lime gelatin infused with the dive-bombing combo of citron vodka, the zest of fresh lime juice, and an electric attitude with blue curaçao.

8 ounces water
One 3-ounce package lime gelatin
5 ounces citron vodka
2 ounces blue curaçao
1 ounce fresh lime juice

MAKES 20 SHOTS ★ SERVES 3 TO 4

1 In a small saucepan, bring the water to a boil.
2 Pour the lime gelatin into a medium heatproof bowl and add the boiling water, stirring until the gelatin is dissolved. Let cool.
3 Add the vodka, curaçao, and lime juice to the cooled mixture, stirring until well combined.
4 Pour mixture into twenty 2-ounce paper or plastic cups and refrigerate. Chill until firm, 4 to 6 hours.

LONG ISLAND EXPRESS

Take the expressway to lala land. Known as the LIE in certain circles (after a few of these, the abbreviated version comes in handy), this is my rendition of the classic Long Island Iced Tea packed into one little high-octane lemony citrus shooter, complete with all the usual suspects.

8 ounces water
One 3-ounce package lemon gelatin
1 ounce vodka
1 ounce rum
1 ounce tequila
1 ounce gin
1 ounce Triple Sec
1 ounce fresh lemon juice
A splash of cola

MAKES 20 SHOTS ★ SERVES 3 TO 4

1 In a small saucepan, bring the water to a boil.
2 Pour the lemon gelatin into a medium heatproof bowl and add the boiling water, stirring until the gelatin is dissolved. Let cool.
3 Add the vodka, rum, tequila, gin, Triple Sec, lemon juice, and cola to the cooled mixture, stirring until well combined.
4 Pour mixture into twenty 2-ounce paper or plastic cups and refrigerate. Chill until firm, 4 to 6 hours.

GREEN MUSE

Known as the "green muse" or "green fairy," the notoriously hallucinogenic absinthe is back on the shelf after an eighty-year hiatus (Pernod is a fine substitute if you cannot find Absente). Naturally, anything surrounded in scandal and taboo is the perfect candidate for a gelatin shooter. Proceed with caution—at 110 proof, any more than one or two of these and the green fog may just rematerialize.

12 ounces water
Two ½-ounce envelopes unflavored gelatin
3 tablespoons superfine sugar
4 ounces Absente or Pernod
A few dashes of orange bitters

GARNISH **OPTIONAL**
20 orange peel twists
MAKES 20 SHOTS ★ SERVES 3 TO 4

1   In a small saucepan, bring the water to a boil.
2   Pour the boiling water into a medium heatproof bowl and sprinkle the unflavored gelatin and sugar into the hot water, stirring until the gelatin and sugar are dissolved. Let cool.
3   Add the Absente and orange bitters to the cooled mixture, stirring until well combined.

4 Pour mixture into twenty 2-ounce paper or plastic cups and refrigerate for 15 minutes, or until slightly set.

5 If garnishing, use a chopstick to push the orange peel into each shooter. Chill until firm, 4 to 6 hours.

CITRUS BOUNCE

This has all the great attributes of a puckery, sweet, lemon-drop cocktail, with none of the spill factor. If you prefer a sugar rim for authentic presentation, run a lemon wedge around the rims of the two-ounce cups and then dip each moistened rim in a small plate of superfine sugar.

8 ounces water
One 3-ounce package lemon gelatin
5 ounces citron vodka
3 ounces Cointreau (or other orange liqueur)
MAKES 20 SHOTS ★ SERVES 3 TO 4

1 In a small saucepan, bring the water to a boil.
2 Pour the lemon gelatin into a medium heatproof bowl and add the boiling water, stirring until the gelatin is dissolved. Let cool.
3 Add the vodka and Cointreau to the cooled mixture, stirring until well combined.
4 Pour mixture into twenty 2-ounce paper or plastic cups and refrigerate. Chill until firm, 4 to 6 hours.

PAPA CUBANA

The importance of being Ernest, in this case anyway, will get you a fabulous daiquiri in Cuba! Back in Havana, expatriate writer Ernest Hemingway had a preference for super-potent daiquiris made with grapefruit juice and maraschino liqueur. He may have preferred his daiquiris sugarless, but here is where we part ways—this is a daiquiri shooter after all.

8 ounces water
One 3-ounce package lime gelatin
5 ounces white rum
2 ounces fresh grapefruit juice
1 ounce maraschino liqueur
MAKES 20 SHOTS ★ SERVES 3 TO 4

1 In a small saucepan, bring the water to a boil.
2 Pour the lime gelatin into a medium heatproof bowl and add the boiling water, stirring until the gelatin is dissolved. Let cool.
3 Add the rum, grapefruit juice, and maraschino liqueur to the cooled mixture, stirring until well combined.
4 Pour mixture into twenty 2-ounce paper or plastic cups and refrigerate. Chill until firm, 4 to 6 hours.

VESPER WHISPER

Conjured from the mind of novelist Ian Fleming in *Casino Royale*, the infamous Vesper martini was named after James Bond's doomed double-agent girlfriend, Vesper Lynd. Not only does he substitute vodka in the sacrosanct gin martini, but also replaces the vermouth with Lillet blond, an herbal wine similar to vermouth—and we have suavely suspended it in gelatin.

12 ounces gin
Two ½-ounce envelopes unflavored gelatin
2 ounces vodka
2 ounces Lillet blond

GARNISH OPTIONAL
20 lemon twists
MAKES 20 SHOTS ★ SERVES 3 TO 4

1 In a small saucepan, bring 4 ounces of the gin to a boil.
2 Pour the unflavored gelatin into a medium heatproof bowl and add the boiling gin, stirring until the gelatin is dissolved. Let cool.
3 Add the remaining 8 ounces of gin, the vodka, and Lillet to the cooled mixture, stirring until well combined.

4 Pour mixture into twenty 2-ounce paper or plastic cups and refrigerate for 15 minutes, or until slightly set.

5 If garnishing, use a chopstick to push a lemon twist into each shooter. Chill until firm, 4 to 6 hours.

THE LUXE LIFE

Suave, glamorous, and sparkling effervescence hits the gelatin shooter.

GELISCIOUS DELUXE

Looking for something festive to serve at your next soirée that goes beyond the predictable champagne cocktail? Look no further— the perfect alternative is this sleek and shimmery shooter, with effervescent champagne and the glamorous Goldschlager, bringing its cinnamon-flavored fire and floating gold leaf.

12 ounces water
One 6-ounce package Sparkling White Grape gelatin
14 ounces chilled champagne
3 ounces Goldschlager

GARNISH **OPTIONAL**
½ cup chocolate sprinkles
MAKES 40 SHOTS ★ SERVES 6 TO 8

1   In a small saucepan, bring the water to a boil.
2   Pour the white grape gelatin into a medium heatproof bowl and add the boiling water, stirring until the gelatin is dissolved. Let cool.
3   Add the champagne and Goldschlager to the cooled mixture, stirring until well combined.
4   Pour mixture into forty 2-ounce paper or plastic cups and refrigerate. Chill until firm, 4 to 6 hours.
5   Garnish each cup with a pinch of chocolate sprinkles, if desired, and serve.

BELLINI-ESQUE

One of my favorite champagne cocktails bounces its way into this peachy sweet shooter, and it's just perfect for a Sunday brunch. Transporting the classic elegance of the Bellini into peach gelatin blended with puréed white (or yellow) peaches and prosecco (Italian champagne) is the quickest way to jiggly bliss.

6 ounces water
One 3-ounce package peach gelatin
½ cup peeled, cubed white peach
1 ounce fresh lemon juice
4 ounces chilled prosecco
MAKES 20 SHOTS ★ SERVES 3 TO 4

1 In a small saucepan, bring the water to a boil.

2 Pour the peach gelatin into a medium heatproof bowl and add the boiling water, stirring until the gelatin is dissolved. Let cool.

3 In a blender, combine the cubed peaches and lemon juice and blend until smooth. (Makes about 4 ounces of peach purée.)

4 Add 4 ounces of peach purée to the cooled gelatin mixture, stirring until well combined. Refrigerate for 15 minutes, or until slightly set. Remove from refrigerator and slowly add the prosecco to the mixture, stirring until well combined.

5 Pour mixture into twenty 2-ounce paper or plastic cups and refrigerate. Chill until firm, 4 to 6 hours.

VIOLET APHRODISIAC

Once frequently served in a few of the more refined brothels of Paris, Parfait Amour is a violet-hued aromatic liqueur that was believed by many to bring on libido-stimulating properties. Double the recipe for a crowd and be sure to serve these up from some novelty ice cube trays with fun, erotic shapes.

12 ounces Parfait Amour liqueur
Two ½-ounce envelopes unflavored gelatin
1 tablespoon superfine sugar
3 ounces vodka
1 ounce Cointreau

GARNISH **OPTIONAL**
20 freshly picked edible violets or orange nasturtiums
MAKES 20 SHOTS ★ SERVES 3 TO 4

1 In a small saucepan, bring 4 ounces of the Parfait Amour to a boil.

2 Pour the unflavored gelatin and sugar into a medium heatproof bowl and add the boiling liqueur, stirring until the gelatin and sugar are dissolved. Let cool.

3 Add the remaining 8 ounces of Parfait Amour, vodka, and Cointreau to the cooled mixture, stirring until well combined.

4   Pour mixture into twenty 2-ounce paper or plastic cups and refrigerate for 15 minutes, or until slightly set.
5   Use a chopstick to push a violet into the top of each cup, if desired. Chill until firm, 4 to 6 hours.

COCOA COGNAC-A-GO-GO

This is one sparkling, energized popper full of extroverted flavors and urban sophistication. It's a perfect blend of heady, rich cognac, Godiva chocolate liqueur (deep chocolate flavor with a hint of orange and mint), Sparkling Mandarin Orange gelatin, and an effervescence from Orangina, a sparkling orange beverage.

14 ounces water

One 6-ounce package Sparkling Mandarin Orange gelatin (or orange gelatin)

6 ounces cognac

4 ounces Godiva liqueur (or crème de cacao)

6 ounces Orangina (or other sparkling orange beverage)

GARNISH **OPTIONAL**

¼ cup lime zest

MAKES 40 SHOTS ★ SERVES 6 TO 8

1 In a small saucepan, bring the water to a boil.

2 Pour the orange gelatin into a medium heatproof bowl and add the boiling water, stirring until the gelatin is dissolved. Let cool.

3 Add the cognac, Godiva liqueur, and sparkling orange beverage to the cooled mixture, stirring until well combined.

4 Pour mixture into forty 2-ounce paper or plastic cups or three plastic ice cube trays, and refrigerate for 15 minutes or until slightly set.

5 Sprinkle a pinch of lime zest onto each cup, if desired. Chill until firm, 4 to 6 hours.

SANGRILA SLIDER

A fruity shot Carmen Miranda could definitely wiggle to, this compact sangria combines ambrosial pear purée and Muscat wine for a slider so luscious you might be tempted to serve it in a parfait glass.

6 ounces water
One 6-ounce box Sparkling White Grape gelatin
One ½-ounce envelope unflavored gelatin
2 ounces fresh orange juice
½ cup peeled, cubed ripe pear
5 ounces Muscat wine
4 ounces club soda

GARNISH **OPTIONAL**
½ cup orange zest
MAKES 30 SHOTS ★ SERVES 6 TO 8

1 In a small saucepan, bring the water to a boil.
2 Pour the white grape and unflavored gelatins into a medium heat-proof bowl and add the boiling water, stirring until the gelatin is dissolved. Let cool.
3 In a blender, combine the orange juice and cubed pears and purée until smooth. (Makes 5 ounces of pear purée).
4 Add the puréed pear mixture and Muscat wine to the cooled gelatin mixture, stirring until well combined.
5 Refrigerate for 15 minutes, or until slightly set. Remove from the refrigerator and add the club soda, stirring until well combined.
6 Pour mixture into thirty 2-ounce paper or plastic cups. Top each cup with a pinch of orange zest, if desired. Chill until firm, 4 to 6 hours.

CITRON SPARKLER

Pucker up, baby, and get ready for a zinger that will send you straight to citrus heaven. Refreshing and bubbly, it's a citrusy shooter that's simultaneously sweet and tart, with a splash of Galliano, an Italian liqueur that adds a whisper of anise, licorice, and vanilla.

8 ounces water
One 3-ounce package lemon gelatin
⅓ cup lemon sorbet
1 ounce Galliano
4 ounces chilled champagne
MAKES 20 SHOTS ★ SERVES 3 TO 4

1 In a small saucepan, bring the water to a boil.

2 Pour the lemon gelatin into a medium heatproof bowl and add the boiling water, stirring until the gelatin is dissolved.

3 Add the lemon sorbet, stirring until dissolved. Let cool.

4 Add the Galliano and champagne to the cooled mixture, stirring until well combined.

5 Pour mixture into twenty 2-ounce paper or plastic cups and refrigerate. Chill until firm, 4 to 6 hours.

CELEBRATION JIGGLES

Festive jiggly shooters to mellow out those holiday celebrations.

CHOCOLATE KIR ROYALE

You can either prepare the predictable Valentine's Day fare of dipping strawberries into chocolate for your sweetie, or you can show off your ultra-clever, modernistic, swanky side and infuse all those romantic elements (including the champagne and flowers) into one over-the-top shot.

6 ounces water
One 3-ounce package strawberry gelatin
2 ounces crème de cassis
2 ounces white crème de cacao
2 ounces chocolate milk
2 ounces chilled champagne

GARNISH OPTIONAL
1 cup whipped cream
5 to 6 freshly picked and rinsed, edible violets or pink tea rose petals

MAKES 4 LARGE OR 20 SMALL SHOTS ★ SERVES 2 TO 6

1 In a small saucepan, bring the water to a boil.
2 Pour the strawberry gelatin into a medium heatproof bowl and add the boiling water, stirring until the gelatin is dissolved. Let cool.
3 Add the crème de cassis, crème de cacao, chocolate milk, and champagne to the cooled mixture, stirring until well combined.

4 Pour mixture into four champagne flutes (or twenty 2-ounce paper or plastic cups) and refrigerate. Chill until firm, 4 to 6 hours.

5 After the gelatin mixture is set, top each serving with a dollop of whipped cream and a few violets or rose petals on top of the whipped cream, if desired, and serve.

ROCKET'S RED ZING

This stars-and-stripes extravaganza is packed with an all-American excess of summer berry zing. Multilayered in red, white, and blue strata, this shimmering shot has enough punch to fuel a bottle rocket and enough flavor to set off a mouthful of fireworks that are well worth the effort.

FIRST LAYER
6 ounces water
One 3-ounce package raspberry gelatin
5 ounces black currant vodka
½ cup fresh or frozen (thawed and rinsed) raspberries

SECOND LAYER
2 ounces cold water
Two 1/2-ounce envelopes unflavored gelatin
4 ounces half-and-half
1/2 cup sugar
1 teaspoon vanilla extract
1/2 cup whipped cream

THIRD LAYER
6 ounces water
Half of a 6-ounce box (¼ cup) Berry Blue gelatin
5 ounces black currant vodka
½ cup fresh or frozen (thawed and rinsed) blueberries

MAKES ABOUT 30 LAYERED SHOTS ★ SERVES 6 TO 8

1. **To make the first layer:** In a small saucepan, bring the water to a boil.
2. Pour the raspberry gelatin into a medium heatproof bowl and add the boiling water, stirring until the gelatin is dissolved. Let cool.
3. Add the vodka to the cooled mixture, stirring until well combined. Stir in the raspberries and pour into a 9-x-13-inch pan. Refrigerate until slightly set, about 15 minutes or until the next layer is ready to add.
4. **To make the second layer:** Pour the cold water in a medium heatproof bowl and sprinkle the unflavored gelatin over the top to soften.
5. In a small saucepan, combine the half-and-half and sugar. Bring to a low boil, stirring constantly.
6. Add the boiling cream and sugar mixture and the vanilla to the softened unflavored gelatin, stirring until well combined. Let cool.
7. Fold the whipped cream into the cooled mixture until well combined. Spoon the mixture over the berry layer in the pan. Return pan to the refrigerator and chill until the next layer is ready to add, about 15 minutes.
8. **To make third layer:** In a small saucepan, bring the water to a boil.
9. Pour the Berry Blue gelatin into a medium heatproof bowl and add the boiling water, stirring until the gelatin is dissolved. Let cool.
10. Add the vodka and blueberries to the cooled mixture, stirring until well combined.
11. Spoon the mixture over the cream layer. Refrigerate and chill until firm, 3 to 4 hours.
12. Cut into 2-inch squares or use a star-shaped cookie cutter, pressing all the way to bottom, to cut out star-shaped shots.

DARK SHADOW SHOOTER

Here's a murky dark shooter conjured from the voodoo whammy of Blavod black vodka, casting its chiaroscuro spell over the creepy floating grape eyeballs in a burst of fruit flavor. This won't win any special effects awards in Hollywood, but the mere power of suggestion will be enough for that moment of thrilling hesitation.

12 ounces water
One 3-ounce package grape gelatin
One 3-ounce package orange gelatin
8 ounces Blavod black vodka
4 ounces crème de cassis

GARNISH `OPTIONAL`
30 grapes (peeled for best eyeball effect)
MAKES 30 SHOTS ★ SERVES 4 TO 6

1 In a small saucepan, bring the water to a boil.
2 Pour the grape and orange gelatins into a medium heatproof bowl and add the boiling water, stirring until the gelatin is dissolved. Let cool.
3 Add the vodka and crème de cassis to the cooled mixture, stirring until well combined.

4 Pour mixture into thirty 2-ounce paper or plastic cups and refrigerate for 15 minutes, or until slightly set.

5 Use a chopstick to push a grape into the center of each cup, if desired. Chill until firm, 4 to 6 hours.

WILD IRISH RICK-O-SHAY

St. Pat's Day just wouldn't be complete without a celebratory shot of Irish whiskey enveloped in lush Emerald Isle green. Jiggling and jovial, this mischievous leprechaun of a shooter is packed with enough potent and creamy chocolate-minty flavor to bring on a thick Irish brogue with a bit of the old Irish mist in yer eye.

1 cup water
One 3-ounce package lime gelatin
4 ounces Irish whiskey (such as Jameson)
2 ounces Bailey's Irish Creme
1 ounce white chocolate liqueur (or white crème de cacao)
1 ounce crème de menthe
MAKES 20 SHOTS ★ SERVES 3 TO 4

1 In a small saucepan, bring the water to a boil.
2 Pour the lime gelatin into a medium heatproof bowl and add the boiling water, stirring until the gelatin is dissolved. Let cool.
3 Add the Irish whiskey, Bailey's, chocolate liqueur, and crème de menthe to the cooled mixture, stirring until well combined.
4 Pour mixture into twenty 2-ounce paper or plastic cups and refrigerate. Chill until firm, 4 to 6 hours.

COQUITO NOG SHOT

Chase away those gray winter days with this creamy south-of-the-border-style nog shot. A Puerto Rican holiday favorite, coquitos are a blend of coconut, the tropical warmth of rum, and eggnog for a festive alternative to the predictable holiday party fare. ¡Feliz Navidad!

8 ounces eggnog
Two ½-ounce envelopes unflavored gelatin
5 ounces white rum
2 ounces Thai coconut milk
½ teaspoon vanilla extract
A pinch of ground cloves
A pinch of ground cinnamon

MAKES 20 SHOTS ★ SERVES 3 TO 4

1 In a small saucepan, bring the eggnog to a low simmering boil.

2 Pour the hot eggnog into a medium heatproof bowl and add the unflavored gelatin, sprinkling it over the top. Let sit for a minute and then stir until the gelatin is dissolved. Let cool.

3 Add the rum, coconut milk, vanilla extract, clove, and cinnamon to the cooled mixture, stirring until well combined.

4 Pour mixture into twenty 2-ounce paper or plastic cups and refrigerate. Chill until firm, 4 to 6 hours.

PEPPERMINT POPPERS

Reminiscent of all those Christmas holidays spent sucking on candy canes, this is a joyous return to our youthful sweet tooth that's spiked with a very adult twist. It's made with the intense mintiness of Rumple Minze, the king of peppermint schnapps, to bring holiday cheer to a roomful of overstressed shoppers.

FIRST LAYER
8 ounces water
Two 1/2-ounce envelopes unflavored gelatin
4 ounces vodka
3 ounces Rumple Minze

SECOND LAYER
8 ounces water
One 3-ounce package cranberry-raspberry gelatin
4 ounces cinnamon schnapps
4 ounces vodka
MAKES ABOUT 30 LAYERED SHOTS ★ SERVES 6 TO 8

1 **To make the first layer:** In a small saucepan, bring water to a boil.
2 Pour the boiling water into a medium heatproof bowl. Sprinkle the unflavored gelatin over the top and stir until the gelatin is dissolved. Let cool.
3 Add the vodka and Rumple Minze to the cooled mixture, stirring until well combined.

4 Spoon 2 tablespoons of the mixture into each of the thirty 2-ounce paper or plastic cups. Refrigerate until slightly set, about 15 minutes.

5 **To make the second layer:** In a small saucepan, bring the water to a boil.

6 Pour the cranberry-raspberry gelatin into a medium heatproof bowl and add the boiling water, stirring until the gelatin is dissolved. Let cool.

7 Add the cinnamon schnapps and vodka to the cooled mixture, stirring until well combined.

8 Spoon 2 tablespoons of the cranberry-raspberry gelatin mixture into each of the cups of Rumple Minze gelatin mixture. Refrigerate and chill until firm, 4 to 6 hours.

NEW YEAR'S FIZZ

What could be more appropriate than to bring in the new year with a nuevo twist on the traditional bit of bubbly cheer? This compact little gem captures all the effervescence and festive flavors of a celebratory champagne punch in a frothy, fizzy shooter.

14 ounces water
One 6-ounce package Sparkling White Grape gelatin
2 ounces cranberry juice
1 ounce maraschino liqueur
2 ounces Triple Sec
2 ounces brandy
1 ounce fresh lemon juice
8 ounces pink spumante (or other champagne)

GARNISH `OPTIONAL`
¼ cup lemon zest
¼ cup tiny confectioner's silver balls
MAKES 40 SHOTS ★ SERVES 6 TO 8

1 In a small saucepan, bring the water to a boil.
2 Pour the white grape gelatin into a medium heatproof bowl and add the boiling water, stirring until the gelatin is dissolved. Let cool.
3 Add the cranberry juice, maraschino liqueur, Triple Sec, brandy, and lemon juice to the cooled mixture, stirring until well combined. Refrigerate for 15 minutes or until slightly set.

4 Remove from refrigerator and add the champagne, stirring until well combined.

5 Pour mixture into forty 2-ounce paper or plastic cups and top each with a pinch of lemon zest and silver balls, if desired. Chill until firm, 4 to 6 hours.

TROPICAL TYPHOONS

A potent taste of paradise in two-ounce cubes
on a wave beyond fruit punch.

MAI TAI FINE

Here's a tropical classic from Trader Vic's, and if his Tiki bars were still in business, I'm sure these little cubes of rummy island bliss would be a favorite on his cocktail menu. Made with light and dark rums, citrus flavors of orange and lime, and the key ingredient to a great Mai Tai—the almond-flavored orgeat syrup.

8 ounces water

One 3-ounce package orange gelatin

4 ounces Barbencourt rum

2 ounces Meyer's dark rum

1 ounce fresh lime juice

½ ounce orgeat syrup (or ½ teaspoon almond extract)

GARNISH OPTIONAL

20 edible flowers (tiny orchids, violets, or nasturtiums)

MAKES 20 SHOTS ★ SERVES 3 TO 4

1 In a small saucepan, bring the water to a boil.

2 Pour the orange gelatin into a medium heatproof bowl and add the boiling water, stirring until the gelatin is dissolved. Let cool.

3 Add the rums, lime juice, and orgeat syrup to the cooled mixture, stirring until well combined.

4 Pour mixture into an 8- or 9-inch square pan and refrigerate. Chill until firm, 4 to 6 hours.

5 Cut into 1½-inch square cubes. If garnishing, place an edible flower on top of each cube, pressing slightly to set into gelatin, and serve.

LULU ON THE BEACH

Don't bother with Prozac! Throw away your Zoloft. I've made a shooter with instant sunny disposition built right in! Intense flavors of pineapple (the nonprescription, all natural antidepressant), orange sorbet, and coconutty Malibu rum transport you to sunny, tropical bliss—yummy!

6 ounces water
One 3-ounce box pineapple gelatin
½ cup mandarin or orange sorbet
5 ounces Malibu coconut-flavored rum
MAKES 20 SHOTS ★ SERVES 3 TO 4

1 In a small saucepan, bring the water to a boil.

2 Pour the pineapple gelatin into a medium heatproof bowl and add the boiling water, stirring until the gelatin is dissolved.

3 Add the mandarin sorbet, stirring until dissolved. Let cool.

4 Add the Malibu rum to the cooled mixture, stirring until well combined.

5 Pour mixture into twenty 2-ounce paper or plastic cups and refrigerate. Chill until firm, 4 to 6 hours.

SOUTH SEAS SHIMMY

Riding on the wave of this transparent blue liquid is a sea of fantastic flavors kissed by a tropical sun. Serve this up single shot style, or dazzle the gang with a Captain Nemo theme. Just fill a glass goldfish bowl with gelatin and, after chilling it to a slightly thickened consistency, add brilliant gummy fish to the depths of your luminous blue underwater aquarium.

16 ounces water

One 3-ounce package Berry Blue gelatin

One 3-ounce box lime gelatin

8 ounces rum, tequila, or vodka

4 ounces blue curaçao

4 ounces Midori

GARNISH **OPTIONAL**

40 gummy fish and worms

MAKES 40 SHOTS ★ SERVES 6 TO 8

1 In a small saucepan, bring the water to a boil.

2 Pour the Berry Blue and lime gelatins into a medium heatproof bowl and add the boiling water, stirring until the gelatin is dissolved. Let cool.

3 Add the rum, blue curaçao, and Midori to the cooled mixture, stirring until well combined.

4   Pour mixture into forty 2-ounce paper or plastic cups and refrigerate for
    15 minutes, or until slightly set.

5   If garnishing, use a chopstick to push a gummy fish or worm into the
    center of each shooter. Chill until firm, 4 to 6 hours.

PIÑA GELATA

All the decadence of a piña colada in a glimmering little shooter. Island-scented with coconut, rum, and pineapple juice, it's enough to send your palate straight to paradise. Thai coconut milk can be found in the ethnic food section of your supermarket or in Asian markets.

8 ounces water
One 3-ounce package pineapple gelatin
5 ounces rum
1½ ounces Thai coconut milk
1 ounce pineapple juice
1 ounce fresh lime juice

GARNISH OPTIONAL
20 paper cocktail umbrellas
MAKES 20 SHOTS ★ SERVES 3 TO 4

1 In a small saucepan, bring the water to a boil.
2 Pour the pineapple gelatin into a medium heatproof bowl and add the boiling water, stirring until the gelatin is dissolved. Let cool.

3 Add the rum, coconut milk, pineapple juice, and lime juice to the cooled
   mixture, stirring until well combined.
4 Pour mixture into twenty 2-ounce paper or plastic cups and refrigerate.
   Chill until firm, 4 to 6 hours. Garnish each shot with a paper umbrella,
   if desired.

TEQUITA BANANA

This swinging combo of tequila and banana liqueur will have you happily enveloped in a fragrant tropical banana haze, while searching for a chandelier to swing from.

8 ounces water
2 tablespoon brown sugar
3 tablespoons instant banana cream
   pudding mix
Two ½-ounce envelopes unflavored gelatin
4 ounces Reposado tequila
2 ounces banana liqueur
1 tablespoon fresh lime juice

MAKES 20 SHOTS ★ SERVES 3 TO 4

1 In a small saucepan, bring the water to a boil.
2 Pour the brown sugar, pudding mix, and unflavored gelatin into a medium heatproof bowl and stir to combine. Add the boiling water, stirring until the brown sugar and gelatin are dissolved. Let cool.
3 Add the tequila, banana liqueur, and lime juice to the cooled mixture, stirring until well combined.
4 Pour mixture into twenty 2-ounce paper or plastic cups and refrigerate. Chill until firm, 4 to 6 hours.

MONSOON MANGO LASSI

Travel to a taste where East meets West. Straight from the streets of Bombay, this cooling, fragrant mix of Indian flavors will envelop your senses like a warm monsoon downpour.

8 ounces water
One 3-ounce package peach gelatin
One ½-ounce envelope unflavored gelatin
2 ounces mango nectar
¼ cup frozen vanilla yogurt
4 ounces gin
½ teaspoon vanilla extract
A pinch of cardamom
4 to 6 fresh mint leaves, finely chopped
MAKES 20 SHOTS ★ SERVES 3 TO 4

1   In a small saucepan, bring the water to a boil.
2   Pour the peach and unflavored gelatins into a medium heatproof bowl and add the boiling water, stirring until the gelatin is dissolved. Let cool.
3   Add the mango nectar, frozen yogurt, gin, vanilla extract, cardamom, and mint to the cooled mixture, stirring until well combined.
4   Pour mixture into twenty 2-ounce paper or plastic cups and refrigerate. Chill until firm, 4 to 6 hours.

EXOTIC-A-GO-GO

Launching the gelatin shot into a whole other stratosphere.

LOTUS DROP

Conjuring the fragrant aroma of ripe plums, this heady shot is made with sweet, fresh plum purée and the nutty tones of Armagnac, the cognac-like French brandy brandishing a typhoon-like potency. Fresh, ripe plums are ideal of course, but if out of season, frozen plums will work fine and are found in most Asian or Latin markets.

PLUM PURÉE
1/2 cup peeled, diced ripe plums
1 tablespoon fresh lime juice

8 ounces water
One 3-ounce package grape gelatin
4 ounces Armagnac (or other brandy)

GARNISH **OPTIONAL**
20 tiny, green, edible orchids

MAKES **20 SHOTS** ★ SERVES **3 TO 4**

1 **To make the plum purée:** In a blender or food processor, combine the plums and lime juice. Blend until puréed and smooth. Makes about 4 ounces.

2 In a small saucepan, bring the water to a boil.

3 Pour the grape gelatin into a medium heatproof bowl and add the boiling water, stirring until the gelatin is dissolved. Let cool.

4 Add the Armagnac and plum purée to the cooled mixture, stirring until well combined.

5 Pour mixture into twenty 2-ounce paper or plastic cups and refrigerate. Chill until firm, 4 to 6 hours. Garnish by gently pressing an orchid into each cup, if desired, and serve.

SAKE SLIDER

This Pan-Asian pearl melds the delicate flavors of sake with a spicy snap of ginger, for an aromatic whisper of Asia enveloped in a slider of pure translucent minimalism. ★ Ginger syrup is easy to make and great to have on hand, but for a shortcut you can pick up premade ginger syrup in most natural-food or Asian markets.

8 ounces sake
Two ½-ounce envelopes unflavored gelatin
6 ounces ginger syrup (page 23)

GARNISH `OPTIONAL`
20 small edible flowers (borage petals, nasturtiums, or
   orange blossoms)
MAKES 20 SHOTS ★ SERVES 3 TO 4

1 Pour 2 ounces of the sake into a medium heatproof bowl and sprinkle the unflavored gelatin over the top to soften.

2 In a small saucepan, bring the ginger syrup to a low boil. Add the heated syrup to the gelatin mixture, stirring until the gelatin is dissolved. Let cool.

3 Add the remaining 6 ounces of sake to the cooled mixture, stirring until well combined.

4 Pour the mixture into twenty 2-ounce paper or plastic cups and refrigerate. Chill until firm, 4 to 6 hours. Garnish each cup with a flower, if desired, and serve.

STALIN'S KISS

OK, the Cold War may be over, but for nostalgia's sake, we have con-jured up this revolutionary little "red square" that looks sparse and compact, but is spiked with Blavod black vodka and the ruby red of sweet blood orange juice. Invite a few comrades over for a stinger of a kiss that has a hidden agenda.

8 ounces water
One 3-ounce package black cherry gelatin
5 ounces Blavod black vodka
3 ounces fresh blood orange or navel orange juice
MAKES 20 SHOTS ★ SERVES 3 TO 4

1 In a small saucepan, bring the water to a boil.
2 Pour the black cherry gelatin into a medium heatproof bowl and add the boiling water, stirring until the gelatin is dissolved. Let cool.
3 Add the black vodka and blood orange juice to the cooled mixture, stirring until well combined.
4 Pour mixture into twenty 2-ounce paper or plastic cups and refriger-ate. Chill until firm, 4 to 6 hours.

PRIMORDIAL OOZE

Here's your chance to get creative with this edible cocktail and impress (or alienate) all your friends. Yes, it may end up looking like a sixth grade science project, but this one has a spiked zoom factor that's positively atomic. Complete with gummy dinosaurs for the full primordial dioramic effect, and if you must go all out you can always make palm trees from lime peel twists and a hot lava river of Red Hots.

24 ounces water
One 6-ounce package lime gelatin
One 3-ounce package cherry gelatin
Half of a 6-ounce package (½ cup) Berry Blue gelatin
10 ounces pepper vodka
4 ounces Midori
½ cup softened vanilla ice cream

GARNISH OPTIONAL
12 to 24 gummy dinosaurs
MAKES ABOUT 24 SHOTS ★ SERVES 4 TO 5

1 In a small saucepan, bring the water to a boil.
2 Pour the lime, cherry, and Berry Blue gelatins into a large heatproof bowl and add the boiling water, stirring until the gelatin is dissolved. Let cool.

3 Add the pepper vodka, Midori, and ice cream to the cooled mixture, stirring until well combined.

4 Pour mixture into a 9-x-13-inch glass pan and refrigerate for 15 minutes, or until slightly set. Place the gummy dinosaurs every few inches, if desired, pressing them into the gelatin just enough to stand upright. Chill until firm, 4 to 6 hours.

5 Dip the bottom of the pan in warm water for about 15 seconds to loosen. Cut into 2–inch squares and serve.

BALINESE SNOWFLAKE

Inspired by the abundance of exotic flavors found on the island of Bali is a lush shooter made with fragrant papaya nectar, mandarin orange, and enhanced with aromatic coconut, for a transcendent experience that is as magical on your tongue as a snowfall in the tropics.

12 ounces water
One 6-ounce package Sparkling Mandarin Orange gelatin
5 ounces gin
5 ounces club soda
4 ounces papaya nectar
4 ounces Thai coconut milk

GARNISH **OPTIONAL**
½ cup Bakers unsweetened coconut flakes
40 tiny, pink, edible orchid blossoms
MAKES 40 SHOTS ★ SERVES 6 TO 8

1 In a small saucepan, bring the water to a boil.
2 Pour the orange gelatin into a medium heatproof bowl and add the boiling water, stirring until the gelatin is dissolved. Let cool.
3 Add the gin, club soda, papaya nectar, and coconut milk to the cooled mixture, stirring until well combined.
4 Pour mixture into forty 2-ounce paper or plastic cups. Sprinkle the top of each cup with coconut flakes, if desired, and refrigerate. Chill until firm, 4 to 6 hours. Garnish each cup with a tiny orchid, if desired, and serve.

CAPPUCCINO KICKER

This thick and creamy kicker is the quickest trip to a late afternoon energy boost; the perfect Rx to blast you out of your 4:00 fits of fatigue. With a jolt of rich and aromatic mocha and cappuccino flavors, this will keep you wired and ready for anything.

3 ounces espresso or strong coffee

4 ounces half-and-half

1 tablespoon chocolate syrup

A dash of ground cinnamon

Two ½-ounce envelopes unflavored gelatin

3 ounces vodka

2 ounces Kahlúa

2 ounces crème de cacao

MAKES 20 SHOTS ★ SERVES 3 TO 4

1 In a small saucepan, combine the espresso, half-and-half, chocolate syrup, and cinnamon over medium heat, stirring until well combined. Bring the mixture to a low boil.

2 Pour unflavored gelatin into a medium heatproof bowl and add the heated espresso mixture, stirring until the gelatin is dissolved. Let cool.

3 Add the vodka, Kahlúa, and crème de cacao to the cooled mixture, stirring until well combined.

4 Pour mixture into twenty 2-ounce paper or plastic cups and refrigerate. Chill until firm, 4 to 6 hours.

THE GEL-X-FILES

Envelope-pushing poppers and risky concoctions
for the young and fearless .

FEAR FACTOR SHOTS

Gelatin shots are the ideal translucent vehicle for showcasing daunting ingredients—edible items that one may fear chewing or swallowing —and for the ultimate fearless factor, unflavored gelatin is the only way to go.

Try whipping up a Russian twist on your vodka shooter by blending caviar with your Stoli and suspending it in unflavored gelatin. Or, perhaps you would prefer a fiery tequila and hot chile pepper combo.

Now if you really want to delve into some serious culinary entomophagy (eating of insects), pick up a bag of live crickets, grasshoppers, cicadas, or tomato hornworms at your local pet store or bait shop. Freeze in a plastic bag, and when you are ready to use them, rinse, pat dry, and add to your favorite gelatin shooter recipe for an extra-crunchy protein boost. Apple Pucker or cinnamon schnapps is another great combo with edible insects such as ants or ant eggs.

I do stress that whatever you choose to ingest must be edible, non-toxic, and chewable. So whether you want to look at this as a mini bungee-jumping experience or an edible truth-or-dare game, the thrill is in the shot—who needs pyrotechnics anyway?

LIGHTNING LUGE

This book would not be complete without a big nod to Salt Lake City, Utah. Besides hosting the Winter Olympics, more importantly it's ranked number one in the nation for its Jell-O intake, with lime their favorite flavor. ★ This shooter is equipped with all the attributes of an energized zip down a snow-covered track, if you cannot find Ke Ke Beach, Midori melon liqueur is a great alternative.

8 ounces water
One 3-ounce package lime gelatin
4 ounces vodka
3 ounces lemon-lime Gatorade
1 ounce Ke Ke Beach lime liqueur

GARNISH **OPTIONAL**
¼ cup powdered sugar
MAKES 20 SHOTS ★ SERVES 3 TO 4

1 In a small saucepan, bring the water to a boil.
2 Pour the lime gelatin into a medium heatproof bowl and add the boiling water, stirring until the gelatin is dissolved. Let cool.
3 Add the vodka, Gatorade, and lime liqueur to the cooled mixture, stirring until well combined.
4 Pour mixture into twenty 2-ounce paper or plastic cups and refrigerate. Chill until firm, 4 to 6 hours.
5 If garnishing, sprinkle each cup with a dusting of powdered sugar, and serve.

MESCAL MYSTERY SHOT

For those of you that thrill at the chance to prove your fearlessness with an iron palate—the type that sits through every *Fear Factor* show, annoyingly declaring just how easy eating that Madagascar cockroach looks—you are prime candidates for this quivering, ornery little shooter. ★ This mescal worm shot is a kinder, gentler version of the *Fear Factor* concept. It's perfect for a crowd, with only one random person getting to chew the little potent gem with its legendary hallucinogenic properties.

12 ounces water
8 ounces limeade
Four ½-ounce envelopes unflavored gelatin
   (or one 6-ounce box lime gelatin)
8 ounces mescal (including the worm)
MAKES 40 SHOTS ★ SERVES 6 TO 8

1 In a small saucepan, bring the water to a boil.
2 Pour the limeade and gelatin into a medium heatproof bowl and let sit for a minute.
3 Add the boiling water to the gelatin and limeade mixture, stirring until the gelatin is dissolved. Let cool.
4 Add the mescal to the cooled mixture, stirring until well combined.
5 Pour mixture into forty 2-ounce paper or plastic cups and refrigerate. Chill until firm, about 4 to 6 hours.

THE ENERGIZER

This is pure liquid dynamite—with enough energy to be called atomic, enough stamina to take on Speedy Gonzales, and twice as much fun as any pink bunny. Fueled with Red Bull, the carbonated energy beverage, this party-sized batch of high-octane sliders will blow the lid off your next bash.

16 ounces water
One 3-ounce package cranberry gelatin
One 3-ounce package peach gelatin
8 ounces Southern Comfort
8 ounces Red Bull energy drink
MAKES 40 SHOTS ★ SERVES 6 TO 8

1 In a small saucepan, bring the water to a boil.
2 Pour the cranberry and peach gelatins into a medium heatproof bowl and add the boiling water, stirring until the gelatin is dissolved. Let cool.
3 Add the Southern Comfort and Red Bull to the cooled mixture, stirring until well combined.
4 Pour mixture into forty 2-ounce paper or plastic cups, or three ice cube trays, and refrigerate. Chill until firm, 4 to 6 hours.

WINDEX WIGGLE

This shooter is loosely based on that aquamarine cocktail by the same name, with the electric blue–hued signature ingredient of blue curaçao (the orange-flavored liqueur), for one super industrial-strength shooter—but we can't guarantee there won't be any streaking.

16 ounces water
One 6-ounce package Berry Blue gelatin
8 ounces black currant vodka
4 ounces blue curaçao
3 ounces fresh orange juice
MAKES 40 SHOTS ★ SERVES 6 TO 8

1 In a small saucepan, bring the water to a boil.
2 Pour the Berry Blue gelatin into a medium heatproof bowl and add the boiling water, stirring until the gelatin is dissolved. Let cool.
3 Add the vodka, curaçao, and orange juice to the cooled mixture, stirring until well combined.
4 Pour mixture into forty 2-ounce paper or plastic cups and refrigerate. Chill until firm, 4 to 6 hours.

JOLLY RANCHERO

What happens when your two favorite pastimes of slamming back tequila shots and sucking on puckery, tart candy collide? You end up in a bacchanalian paradise, with a fiery high-octane explosion of flavors that will knock you and your compadres right off those donkeys.

12 ounces water
One 6-ounce package X-treem Apple
   (or watermelon) gelatin
6 ounces tequila
4 ounces Apple Pucker schnapps
4 ounces peach schnapps
3 ounces cranberry juice
MAKES 40 SHOTS ★ SERVES 6 TO 8

1   In a small saucepan, bring the water to a boil.
2   Pour the apple gelatin into a medium heatproof bowl and add the boiling water, stirring until the gelatin is dissolved. Let cool.
3   Add the tequila, apple and peach schnapps, and cranberry juice to the cooled mixture, stirring until well combined.
4   Pour mixture into forty 2-ounce paper or plastic cups and refrigerate. Chill until firm, 4 to 6 hours.

GELAMEISTER

Jagermeister brings to this shooter wonderful bittersweet, spicy, peppery tones, and is an elixir that the Germans claim to be "good for what ails you." Paired with cherry gelatin and some 7-Up for the tum tum, this is one great hair-of-the-dog hangover remedy for whatever bit you the night before.

8 ounces water
One 3-ounce package cherry gelatin
4 ounces 7-Up
3 ounces Jagermeister
MAKES 20 SHOTS ★ SERVES 3 TO 4

1   In a small saucepan, bring the water to a boil.
2   Pour the cherry gelatin into a medium heatproof bowl and add the boiling water, stirring until the gelatin is dissolved. Let cool.
3   Add the 7-Up and Jagermeister to the cooled mixture, stirring until well combined.
4   Pour mixture into twenty 2-ounce paper or plastic cups and refrigerate. Chill until firm, 4 to 6 hours.

WILD RASPBERRY RICKEY

Taking our cues from the classic fizzy cocktail made with lime juice, gin, and club soda, this effervescent gin rickey is going on one wild ride and giving it the raspberry—for a tangy Singapore Sling–like makeover.

6 ounces water
One 3-ounce package raspberry gelatin
5 ounces gin
3 ounces club soda
2 ounces fresh lime juice

GARNISH **OPTIONAL**
¼ cup lime zest
MAKES 20 SHOTS ★ SERVES 3 TO 4

1 In a small saucepan, bring the water to a boil.
2 Pour the raspberry gelatin into a medium heatproof bowl and add the boiling water, stirring until the gelatin is dissolved. Let cool.
3 Add the gin, club soda, and lime juice to the cooled mixture, stirring until well combined.
4 Pour mixture into twenty 2-ounce paper or plastic cups and refrigerate for 15 minutes, or until slightly set.
5 Sprinkle the top of each cup with a pinch of lime zest, if desired. Chill until firm, 4 to 6 hours.

DEDICATION

To Hudson . . . my fabulously creative sister and a fearless partner in the quest for adventure and fun.

ACKNOWLEDGMENTS

Swimming in an endless sea of jiggle-iscious possibilities, I had the great fortune to have expert navigational help and collaboration from more than just a few talented people.

Huge thanks to my editor extraordinaire (ask anyone), Bill LeBlond, for his support and conceptually brilliant and jiggly vision, as well as to the ultra-savvy editing expertise of Assistant Editor Amy Treadwell. Thanks also to the rest of the Chronicle team: Jan Hughes, Doug Ogan, Aya Akazawa, Azi Rad, Beth Steiner, Ann Rolke, and Stella Lai.

Many thanks to my exceptional friends and family, whose moral support and talent for thinking outside of the box (in this case, a box of gelatin) were priceless when it came to all the collaborative brainstorming, feedback on concepts, fearless taste-testing, and editing insights:
Hudson Pierce Rhoads, Geoff Rhoads, Tim Evans, Michele Evans and Tara Boeser, Taylor James Pierce, Masha Turchinsky, June Kang, Lara Turchinsky, Brian Rhoads, Shannon Santos, Alison Nightingale, Mark Nightingale, Bobbie Rhoads, John Magee, Robert Johnson, Bonnie Durance, Phil Seder, Nick Pierce and Donna Peterson, Dirk and Lisa Pierce, Karen Brooks, Lena Lencek, Eduardo Gustamante, Karen Von Clezie, and Scott Bartley.

And finally, to my niece Amanda, and nephews Trevor and Hugo Rhoads, for their expert jiggly insights, based purely on many bowls of yummy, fun gelatin.

MITTIE HELLMICH, a photographer, writer, cocktail creator, and previously the Liquid Assets columnist for the *Oregonian*, is the author and photographer of *Paradise on Ice*. Her work has appeared in *Highballs High Heels* and *Atomic Cocktails,* also from Chronicle Books. She lives in Portland, Oregon.

STELLA LAI, is an award-winning artist and designer based in San Francisco. She currently teaches at the California College of Arts and Crafts.